Cars and Trucks

Written and Illustrated by Karen Rissing

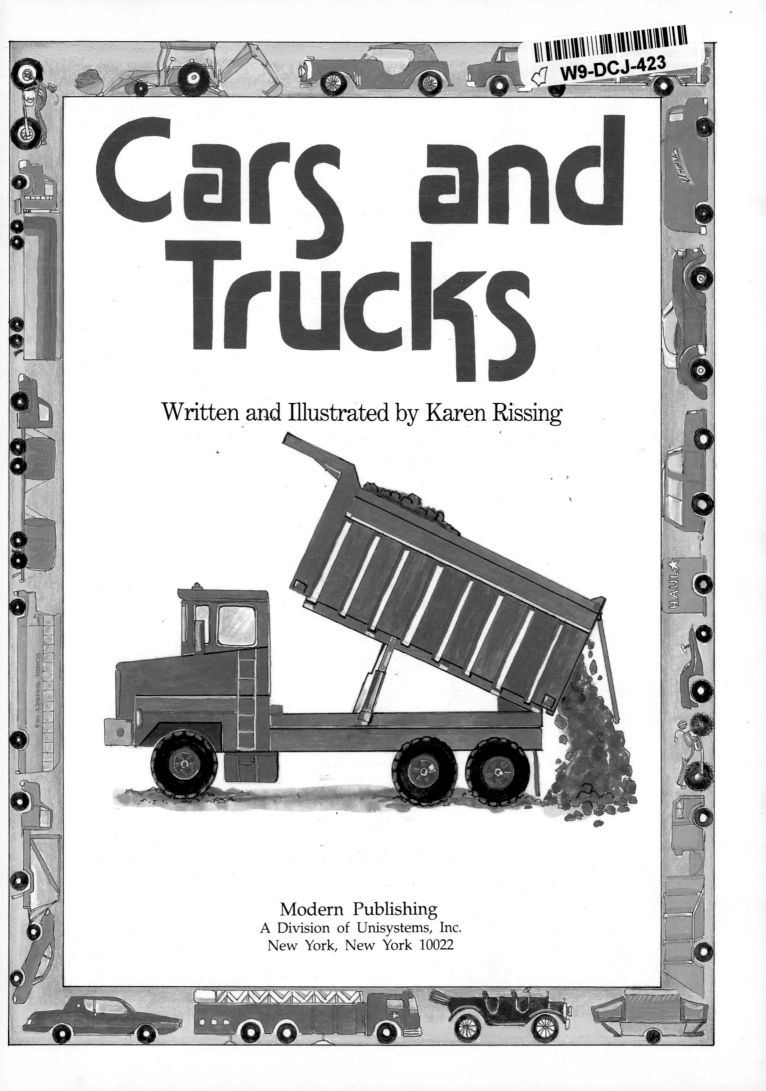

Modern Publishing
A Division of Unisystems, Inc.
New York, New York 10022

Delivery Truck

Tractor

Pickup Truck

School Bus

SCHOOL DISTRICT 7077

Hitch and Harrow

Livestock Truck

Farm trucks haul animals and deliver loads of eggs, milk, hay and many other items. The farmer's tractor starts working the land early in the morning, even before the school bus picks up the children and takes them to school.

**18-Wheel
Tractor Trailer**

Single-Axle Truck

Convertible

Motorcycle

4-Door Sedan

Many kinds of cars and trucks travel on the highway. Delivery trucks bring food and other items from place to place. A convertible is a car with a special roof that folds back. Tractor trailers transport big loads cross-country.

Garbage Truck

Street Sweeper

Cherry Picker Truck

The city is a busy place crowded with cars, trucks and many people. Taxis and buses take people wherever they wish to go. The city street sweeper helps keep the streets clean.

Bus

Taxi Cab

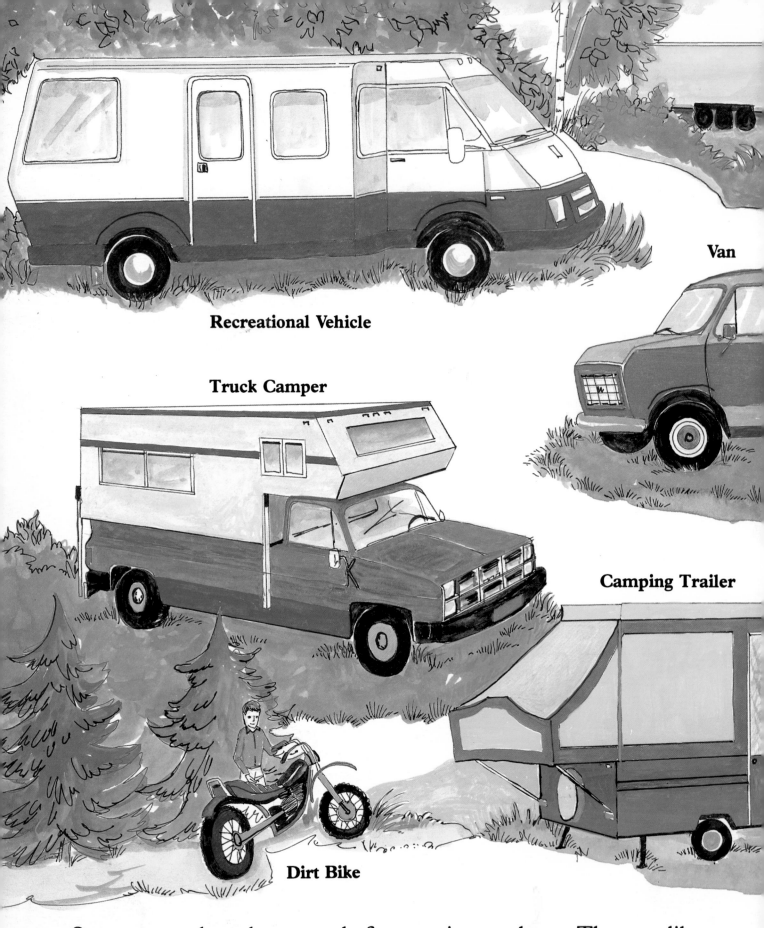

Van

Recreational Vehicle

Truck Camper

Camping Trailer

Dirt Bike

Some cars and trucks are made for camping outdoors. They are like homes on wheels. Dirt bikes, dune buggies and off-road vehicles ride over sandy or bumpy land. Vacationing in a camper or van can be fun. Some people live year round in mobile homes that stay permanently parked in trailer parks.

Mobile Home

Off-Road Vehicles

Cars help people get from place to place. The car carrier truck is large enough to deliver many new cars and vans.

New Car Carrier

**Hot Rod
Funny Car**

Racing Car

RACING TODAY
9-5
HOT ROD SHOW

**Antique
Racing Car**

It's fun to watch racing cars and dragsters zoom around the track.
There are many models of sleek sports cars that are fun to own and
drive, or just to look at.

Fire Engine

Ambulance

Police Car

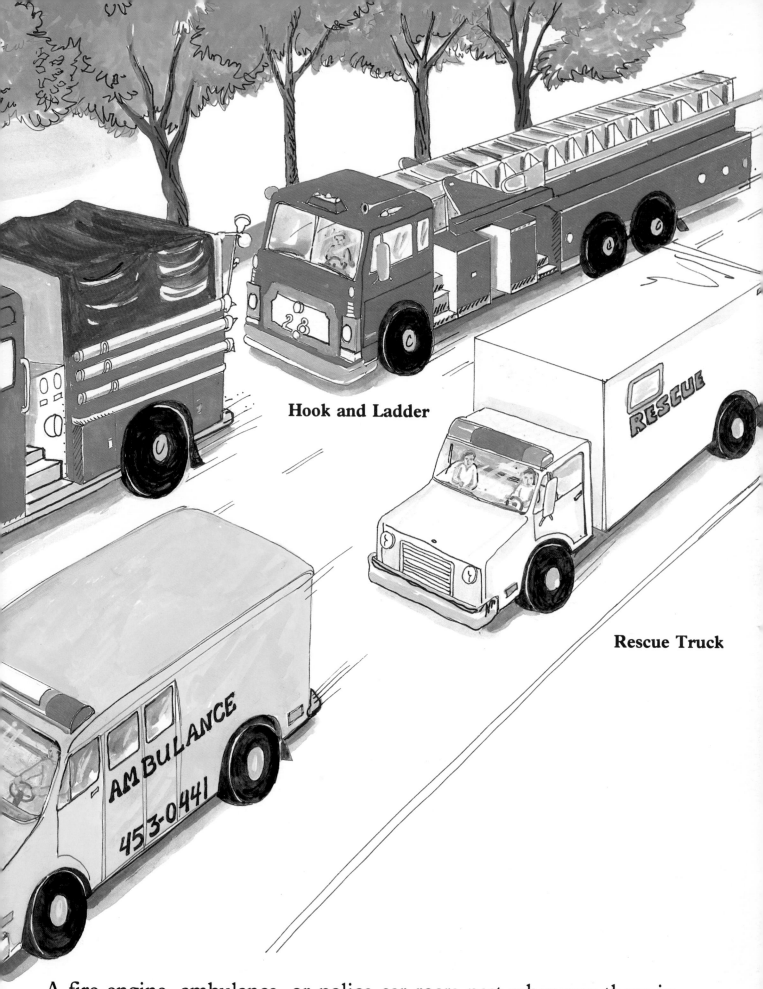

Hook and Ladder

Rescue Truck

A fire engine, ambulance, or police car roars past whenever there is an emergency. Their flashing lights and ringing sirens warn all other cars and trucks that they are driving by.

1937 Jaguar

1910 Model T Ford

1958 Edsel

1962 Cadillac

ANTIQUE
and
CLASSIC
AUTO SHOW

1933 Duesenberg

1965 Mustang

Antique Delivery Truck

1955 Thunderbird

Very old cars are fun! They show us what cars were like years ago. Antique cars or trucks can usually be seen at an auto show or in an automobile museum. Sometimes you'll see an antique car driving down the street!

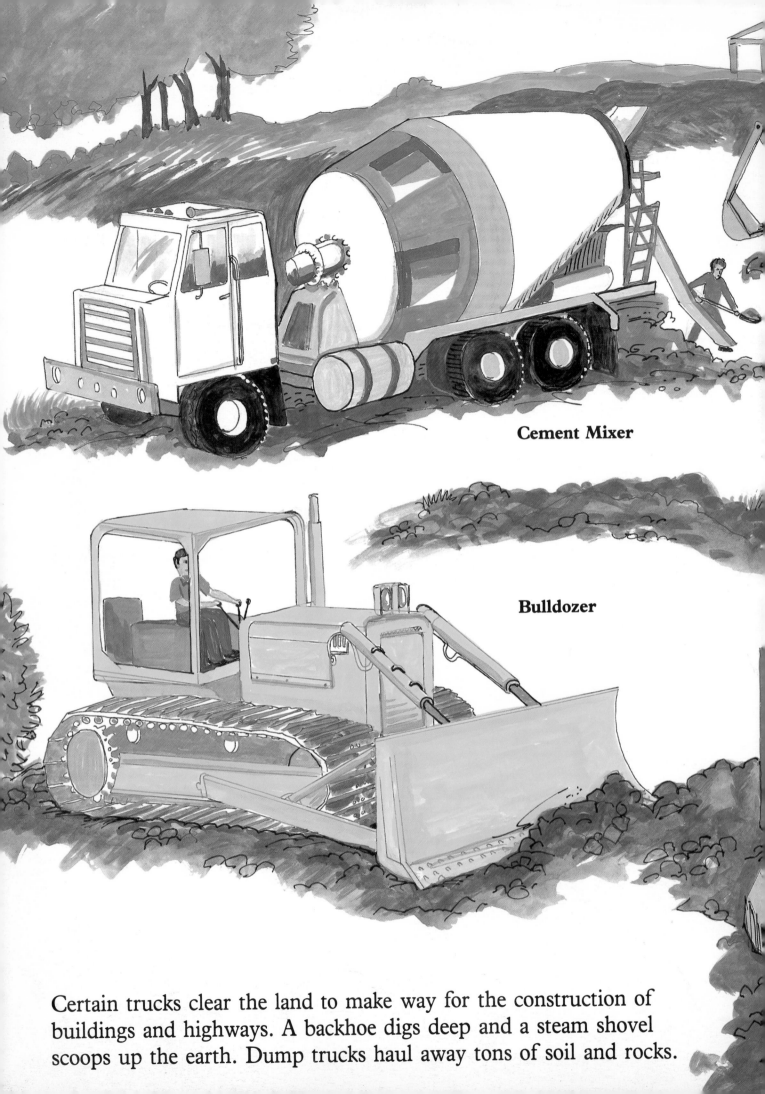

Cement Mixer

Bulldozer

Certain trucks clear the land to make way for the construction of buildings and highways. A backhoe digs deep and a steam shovel scoops up the earth. Dump trucks haul away tons of soil and rocks.

Backhoe

Dump Truck

Steam Shovel Excavator

Moving vans are built to carry the belongings of people moving from one place to another. Smaller pickup trucks also help carry furniture and clothes to a new home. Whether families move across the country or across town, moving vans help you move easily and quickly so that you'll be able to make friends in your new neighborhood right away.

Moving Van

Pickup Truck